Animal Talk

Mexican Folk Art Animal Sounds in English and Spanish

Cynthia Weill
Wood Sculptures from Oaxaca by
Rubí Fuentes and Efraín Broa

Roosters say
COCK-A-DOODLE-DOO
Can you?

Los gallos dicen

KI-KIRI-KI

¿Puedes tú?

What do kitties say?
MEOW MEOW

¿Qué dicen los gatitos?
MIAU MIAU

Fish say
GLUB GLUB

Los peces dicen
GLUB GLUB

Goats say
MEH MEH
Can you?

Las cabras dicen
BEE BEE
¿Puedes tú?

What do tigers say?
GRR GRR!

¿Qué dicen los tigres?
¡GRGRGR GRGRGR!

Cows say
MOO MOO

Las vacas dicen
MU MU

Las abejas dicen
ZUM ZUM
¿Puedes tú?

¿Qué dicen los caballos?

JIII JIII

Dogs say
WOOF WOOF

Los perros dicen
GUAU GUAU

Frogs say
RIBBIT RIBBIT
Can you?

Las ranas dicen

CRUÁ CRUÁ

¿Puedes tú?

What do piggies say?
OINK OINK

¿Qué dicen los puerquitos?

OINC OINC

Lions say
ROAR ROAR!

Los leones dicen
¡RAHR RAHR!

Las serpientes dicen

SSSS SSSS

¿Puedes tú?

Turkeys say
GOBBLE GOBBLE

Los pavos dicen
GORDO GORDO

Owls say

HOO HOO

Can you?

Los búhos dicen

UU UU

¿Puedes tú?

Photo: Jorge Luis Santiago

Rubí Fuentes and Efraín Broa are considered master artisans. Efraín is well known for his elegant figures and Rubí for her delicate and detailed painting. They are members of one of Oaxaca's oldest wood carving families.

Pronunciation Guide

*Cock-a-doodle-doo – Kak-a-du-dul-du	Moo Moo – Mu mu	Oink oink – Oinc oinc
**Ki-kiri-ki – Key-kir-e-key	Mu mu – Moo moo	Oinc onic – Oink oink
Meow meow – Mi-ow mi-ow	Buzz buzz – Bzzz bzzz	Roar roar – Raaar raaar
Miau miau – Mow-mow	Zum zum – Soom soom	Rahr rahr – Raer raer
Glub glub – Glub glub	Neigh neigh – Ne ne	Hiss hiss – Jis jis
Glub glub – Glewb glewb	Jiii jiii – Heee heee	Ssss ssss – Ssss ssss
Meh meh – Me-eee me-eee	Woof woof – Wuf wuf	Gobble gobble – Gaab-el gaab-el
Bee bee – Bay bay	Gua gua – Gwow gwow	Gordo gordo – Gore doh gore doh
Grr Grr – Grr Grr	Ribbet ribbet – Ribet ribet	Hoo hoo – Hu hu
Grgrgr grgrgr – Grr Grr	Cruá cruá – Crewa crewa	Uu uu – Ooo ooo

*pronunciations are best approximation for speakers of Spanish **pronunciations are best approximations for speakers of English

Dedication

To Judith Burton, my dear friend and advisor

Thanks to

Vicky Weill, Nancy Mygatt, Mollie Welsh Kruger, Ruth Borgman, Myriam Chapman, Stephanie and Fernando Villarreal, Anne Mayagoitia, Sandra Aguilar, Hugo Cerón, J. M. Moracho, Janet Glass, Jan Asikainen, Casa Panchita, Amy Mulvihill, Joyce Grossbard, Susan Milligan, The Field Museum, Rocky Behr, Fernando Pedro, Frank Hebert and The Bank Street Writers Lab

Cover and Book Design by

Sergio A. Gómez

Photography: Otto Piron

FIRST EDITION   10 9 8 7 6 5 4 3 2 1
Library of Congress Cataloging-in-Publication Data Names: Weill, Cynthia, author. Title: Animal talk : Mexican folk art animal sounds in English and Spanish /Cynthia Weill ; with hand-carved animal figures by Oaxaca artists, Rubi Fuentes and Efrain Broa. Other titles: Mexican folk art animal sounds in English and Spanish Description: First Edition. | El Paso, TX : Cinco Puntos Press, 2016. | Series: First concepts in mexican folk art | Parallel English and Spanish texts. Identifiers: LCCN 2015024954 | ISBN 9781941026328 (hardback) ISBN 9781941026335 (e-book) Subjects: LCSH: Animal sounds—Juvenile literature. | Animals in art—Juvenile literature. | Folk art—Mexico—Oaxaca (State)—Juvenile literature. | BISAC: JUVENILE NONFICTION / Concepts / Sounds. | JUVENILE NONFICTION / Animals / Lions, Tigers, Leopards, etc.. | JUVENILE NONFICTION / Art / Sculpture. | JUVENILE NONFICTION / Foreign Language Study / Spanish. Classification: LCC QL765 .W45 2016 | DDC 591.59/4—dc23 LC record available at http://lccn.loc.gov/2015024954